THE WEE BOOK O' BURNS
QUOTES FRAE THE BARD

By **Susan Cohen**
Illustrated by **Jane Cornwell**

Text copyright © 2020
Susan Cohen

A CIP record of this book is available from the British Library.

Paperback ISBN 978-1-913237-11-0

First published in the UK in 2020 by The Wee Book Company Ltd.

Printed and bound by Bell & Bain Ltd, Glasgow.

The Bard – A Wee Introduction

If Robert Burns was alive today, he'd be as famous as a rock star. He was one of the best poets that ever there was, and we here in Scotland can claim him to be wan o' wur ain. Aye, it's enough tae make us a' walk an inch or two taller.

Every year people celebrate Burns Night all around the world with parties of poetry, song, haggis, whisky and raucous good humour. Burns Suppers have been cracking on for over 200 years and are now more popular than ever. The man himself would have loved to know that.

There's lots tae love about Robert Burns's work but something that is sure tae strike you is its honesty – he held nothing back. In his work, his life is laid bare and that's why much has been written about the man himself. He was complex and he led a complicated life.

Burns's moods oscillated between the depths of despair, experiencing 'heart-corroding care and grief', and lightly-spun gaiety, declaring that 'I never fash; I rhyme for fun'. Aye, like many of us, catch him on a good day, and he flew. Catch him on a bad day, and his 'luckless lot' was gloomy and there for all to see, right there on his sleeve, with his heart.

Burns's emotional setting was always full on – he appeared to have no edit, no mute button – and it's this that sets his writing ablaze. His genius lay in combining words in ways which managed to describe his great torrents of emotion with eye-watering intensity. Spend a few days/weeks/months reading through his complete works and they'll knock your socks off. That is what this Wee Book hopes to inspire – well, not to have your socks knocked off but to whet your appetite for his work so you won't be able to resist the urge to go exploring, to find out more.

Robert Burns was born into poverty on 25th January, 1759 and rose through graft and 'heaven-taught' gifts, to be the toast of a society which was riding high as the centre of the world's enlightened philosophising. He became the first Scottish Bard and in his short life, achieved so much artistically that he was the first poet to achieve celebrity status in his own lifetime.

From his early years, he had a back-breaking workload on the family farm, something which was to weaken his health. His father, William inspired his formal education and improvement, in contrast to his mother, Agnes who introduced him to the beauty of Scots ballads, songs and folk tales. As a result, Burns started life with a foot in both worlds – English and Scots. He grew up to love the company of friends and of course, he grew up to love the company of the ladies.

He was reputed to be wild, considered almost dangerous, and 'wore the only tied hair in the parish'. He was quite the dandy and seemed to have a good line in patter, described by a friend as having a 'facility in addressing the fair sex'.

It was said that his 'genius or mental power was undoubtedly great' and his published books of poetry changed his life, bringing fame and access to high society.

He went on to marry the brave-hearted Jean Armour, a remarkable woman whom he referred to as the 'jewel' among the local Mauchline Belles. Jean was strong and intelligent. She was also resilient – she had to be, married to Burns.

Burns had financial difficulties and as well as working on the family's rented farm, he took a job as an exciseman. Worn out by hard physical labour and illness, Burns died on the 21st of July, 1796. He was only 37 years old.

Many believe Burns to be one of the most important literary figures in history. There's no doubt that his work is as relevant to us now as it was to his readers then.

We can all identify with the angst-ridden passion of loves won, lost and scorned, and in these days of concerns about climate change, we can all identify with the need to value and respect the natural world. We all feel the same sense of outrage at social, religious and political two-faced hypocrisy, and we still feel a deep compassion for the struggle of the poor trying desperately to feed their families whilst trying to somehow to keep themselves sane. And of course, we identify with his deep-seated love for his ain folk and his ain country, beloved Scotia. Sure we dae!

Debates about how Burns lived his life often rage – quite rightly so, the man caused intense suffering – but what this Wee Book aims to do is to fan the flames of interest for the work he left behind in a way which is easy and accessible fur ivrybody.

This Wee Book doesnae purport to be anything fantoosh and scholarly but rather, it's a wee taster of bite-sized chunks of Burns's quotes, compiled by a fan. Okay, a superfan!

Hopefully by the end of this Wee Book, you'll feel like running oot tae the nearest book shop to get your hands on a copy of his complete works or hoofin' doon to the brilliant Robert Burns Birthplace Museum in Alloway to have a good nosey roond or visitin' anywhere he once was. Yes, dae tha'. Walk in the footsteps of Burns. That can't be anything but an inspiring thing.

Robert Burns, gallus, tortured, radical, vulnerable, callous, sensitive genius – for better or worse, we salute you!

Liberty's in every blow!
Let us do - or die!

Bruce's Address to his Army at Bannockburn

> *"I backward mus'd on wasted time*
> *How I had spent my youthfu' prime,*
> *An' done nae thing,*
> *But stringing blethers up in rhyme,*
> *For fools to sing."*

The Vision

> *"I am nae poet, in a sense;*
> *But just a rhymer like by chance"*

Epistle to J Lapraik

" The simple Bard, unbroke by rules of art,
He pours the wild effusions of the heart;
And if inspir'd 'tis Nature's pow'rs inspire;
Her's all the melting thrill, and her's the kindling fire. "

Motto Prefixed To The Author's First Publication

" For me, I'm on Parnassus' Brink,
Rivin' the words to gar them clink;
Whyles daez't wi' love, whyles daez't wi' drink
Wi jads or Masons,
An' whyles, but ay owre late I think,
Braw sober lessons. "

To Davie – Second Epistle

I like the lasses
- Gude forgie me!

Epistle to J Lapraik

"*O, once I lov'd a bonnie lass,*
Ay, and I love her still;
And whilst that virtue warms my breast,
I'll love my handsome Nell."

Handsome Nell

"*O let me steal one liquid kiss,*
For oh! My soul is parch'd with love."

Delia, An Ode

"*The tyrant Death, with grim control,*
May seize my fleeting breath;
But tearing Peggy from my soul
Must be a stronger death."

Braving Angry Winter's Storms

" *Her eyes are the lightenings of joy and delight:*
Her slender neck, her handsome waist,
Her hair well buckl'd, her stays well lac'd,
Her taper white leg ... "

My girl she's airy, she's buxom and gay

" *Her yellow hair, beyond compare,*
Comes trinkling down her swan white neck,
And her two eyes, like stars in skies,
Would keep a sinking ship frae wreck. "

Mally's Meek, Mally's Sweet

"*No love but thine my heart shall know,*
Fairest maid"

Fairest Maid On Devon Banks

"*For her I'll dare the billow's roar,*
For her I'll trace a distant shore,"

My Highland Lassie, O

"*Wi' mony a vow, and lock'd embrace,*
Our parting was fu' tender;
And, pledging aft to meet again,
We tore oursels asunder;"

Highland Mary

" *For if thou be what I wad hae thee,*
And tak the counsel I shall gie thee,
I'll never rue my trouble wi' thee,
The cost nor shame o't,
But be a loving father to thee,
And brag the name o't. "

A Poet's Welcome to his Love-Begotten Daughter

" *Come weel, come woe, I care na by;*
I'll tak what Heav'n will sen' me, "

My Nanie O

"There was a lass, and she was fair,
At kirk or market to be seen;
When a' our fairest maids were met,
The fairest maid was bonie Jean."

Bonie Jean

"Something, in ilka part o' thee,
To praise, to love, I find,
But dear as is thy form to me,
Still dearer is my mind."

It is Na, Jean, Thy Bonie Face

"Oh Jeany, thou hast stolen away my soul!"

On Jean Armour

SUSAN COHEN

I Love My Jean

Of a' the airts the wind can blaw,
I dearly like the West;
For there the bony Lassie lives,
The Lassie I lo'e best:
There's wild-woods grow, and rivers row,
And mony a hill between;
But day and night my fancy's flight
Is ever wi' my Jean.

I see her in the dewy flowers,
I see her sweet and fair;
I hear her in the tunefu' birds,
I hear her charm the air:
There's not a bony flower that springs
By fountain, shaw, or green;
There's not a bony bird that sings
But minds me o' my Jean.

" Talk not of Love, it gives me pain,
For Love has been my foe;
He bound me with an iron chain,
And plung'd me deep in voice! "

Love in the Guise of Friendship

" No! still I beg a place,
Still near thy heart some little, litte trace,
For that dear trace, the world I would resign,
Oh, let me live – and die – and think it mine! "

Noble Verses By The Bard to Clarinda – on an occasion when
she had said that 'they must part'

Ae Fond Kiss

Ae fond kiss, and then we sever;
Ae fareweel, and then forever!
Deep in heart-wrung tears I'll pledge thee,
Warring sighs and groans I'll wage thee.
Who shall say that Fortune grieves him,
While the star of hope she leaves him?
Me, nae cheerfu' twinkle lights me;
Dark despair around benights me.

I'll ne'er blame my partial fancy,
Naething could resist my Nancy;
But to see her was to love her;
Love but her, and love forever.
Had we never lov'd sae kindly,
Had we never lov'd sae blindly,
Never met – or never parted –
We had ne'er been broken-hearted.

Fare thee weel, thou first and fairest!
Fare thee weel, thou best and dearest!
Thine be ilka joy and treasure,
Peace. enjoyment, love, and pleasure!
Ae fond kiss, and then we sever;
Ae fareweel, alas, forever!
Deep in heart-wrung tears I'll pledge thee,
Warring sighs and groans I'll wage thee!

**"*The courtiers' gems may witness love,*
But, 'tis na love like mine."**

Behold, My Love, How Green The Groves

**"*Gin a body meet a body*
Comin thro' the rye,
Gin a body kiss a body
Need a body cry."**

Comin' Thro' The Rye

"*Love enslaves the man*"

Beware O' Bonie Ann

And let us mind, faint
heart ne'er wan

A lady fair

Epistle To Dr Blacklock

**"*I ask for dearest life alone,
That I may live to love her,*"**

Come, Let Me Take Thee To My Breast

**"*The diamond-dew in her een sae blue,
Where laughing love sae wanton swims.*"**

My Lord A-Hunting

**"*His cheek to hers he aft did lay,
And love was aye the tale*"**

Down The Burn, Davie

"*Love will break the soundest rest*"

Bonie Jean

"*Let love spark in her e'e;*
Let her lo'e nae man but me;"

Love For Love

"*Wi' her I'll blithely bear it,*
And think my lot divine."

My Wife's A Winsome Wee Thing

"*My heart is sair – I dare na tell,*
My heart is sair for Somebody;
I could wake a winter night
For the sake o' Somebody."

For the Sake of Somebody

"*We will big a wee, wee house,*
And we will live like king and queen;
Sae blythe and merry's we will be,
When ye set by the wheel at e'en."

Duncan Davison

"*The tender thrill, the pitying tear,*
The generous purpose nobly dear,
The gentle look that rage disarms —
These are all Immortal charms."

My Peggy's Charms

When chapman billies leave the street,
And drouthy neebors neebors meet,
As market-days are wearing late,
And folk begin to tak the gate;
While we sit bousin, at the nappy,
And gettin fou and unco happy,
We think na on the lang Scots miles,
The mosses, waters, slaps, and stiles,
That lie between us and our hame,
Whare sits our sulky, sullen dame,
Gathering her brows like gathering storm,
Nursing her wrath to keep it warm.

Tam O' Shanter

A Red Red Rose

O my Luve is like a red, red rose
That's newly sprung in June;
O my Luve is like the melody
That's sweetly played in tune.

So fair art thou, my bonnie lass,
So deep in luve am I;
And I will luve thee still, my dear,
Till a' the seas gang dry.

Till a' the seas gang dry, my dear,
And the rocks melt wi' the sun;
I will love thee still, my dear,
While the sands o' life shall run.

And fare thee weel, my only luve!
And fare thee weel awhile!
And I will come again, my luve,
Though it were ten thousand mile.

The heart aye's the part aye
That makes us right or wrang.

Epistle To A Young Friend

"*Courtly grandeur bright*
The fancy may delight,
But never, never can come near the heart"

Mark Yonder Pomp Of Costly Fashion

"*May guardian angels take a spell,*
An' steer you seven miles south o' hell:"

Epistle To James Tennant Of Glenconner

"*The friend we trust, the fair we love –*
And we desire no more"

A Grace After Dinner

"*shelter, shade, nor home have I;*
Save in these arms of thine, Love."

Forlorn, My Love, No Comfort Near

"*Wi' her I'll blithely bear it,*
And think my lot divine."

My Wife's A Winsome Wee Thing

"*Fair and lovely as thou art,*
Thou hast stown my very heart,
I can die – but canna part,
My bonie Dearie."

Ca' The Yowes To The Knowes

John Anderson my Jo

John Anderson my jo, John,
When we were first acquent;
Your locks were like the raven,
Your bony brow was brent;
But now your brow is beld, John,
Your locks are like the snaw;
But blessings on your frosty pow,
John Anderson my Jo.

John Anderson my jo, John,
We clamb the hill the gither;
And mony a canty day, John,
We've had wi' ane anither:
Now we maun totter down, John,
And hand in hand we'll go;
And sleep the gither at the foot,
John Anderson my Jo.

The Slave's Lament

It was in sweet Senegal that my foes did me enthrall
For the lands of Virginia-ginia O;
Torn from that lovely shore, and must never see it more,
And alas! I am weary, weary O!
Torn from that lovely shore, and must never see it more;
And alas! I am weary, weary O!

All on that charming coast is no bitter snow and frost,
Like the lands of Virginia-ginia O:
There streams for ever flow, and there flowers for ever blow,
And alas! I am weary, weary O!
There streams for ever flow, and there flowers for ever blow,
And alas! I am weary, weary O!

The burden I must bear, while the cruel scourge I fear,
In the lands of Virginia-ginia O;
And I think on friends most dear, with the bitter, bitter tear,
And alas! I am weary, weary O!
And I think on friends most dear, with the bitter, bitter tear,
And alas! I am weary, weary O!

" *Life is but a day at most,* "

Written in Friars Carse Hermitage, Nithsdale

" *catch the moments as they fly,*
And use them as ye ought "

A Bottle And A Friend

" *If happiness hae not her seat*
An' centre in the breast,
We may be wise, or rich, or great,
But never can be blest; "

Epistle to Davie, A Brother Poet

" *I live to-day as well's I may, regardless of to-morrow* "

My Father Was A Farmer

**" We'll live a' our days,
And them that comes behin' "**

Hey, Ca' Thro' – Boat Song

**" be merry, I advise;
And as we're merry, may we still be wise. "**

Address Spoken by Miss Fontenelle

**" Pleasure is a wanton trout,
An ye drink it a', ye'll find him out. "**

Gudewife, Count The Lawin

" This life has joys for you and I;
An' joys that riches ne'er could buy, "

Epistle To Davie, A Brother Poet

" When fevers burn, or argues freezes,
Rheumatics gnaw, or colics squeezes,
Our neibor's sympathy can ease us, "

Address To The Toothache

" Here's to them that wish us weel,
May a' that's guid watch o'er 'em! "

O May, Thy Morn

" Rich is the tribute of the grateful mind. "

Inscription To Miss Graham Of Fintry

Content wi' you
to mak a pair,
Whare'er I gang

Epistle To James Smith

" *Are ye hale, and weel and cantie?* **"**

Epistle To Dr Blacklock

" *You'll easy draw a lang-kent face,*
But no sae weel a stranger **"**

Epigram Addressed To An Artist

" *Friendship, mysterious cement of the soul!* **"**

Epistle to James Smith

" *Yours this moment I unseal,*
And faith I'm gay and hearty!
To tell the truth and shame the deil,
I am as fou as Bartie:
But Foorsday, sir, my promise leal
Expect me o' your partie,
If on a beastie I can speel,
Or hurl in a cartie. **"**

Epistle to James Smith

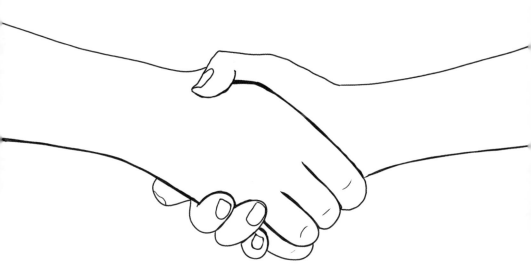

" *He'll hae misfortunes great an' sma',*
But aye a heart aboon them a',
He'll be a credit till us a'–
We'll a' be proud o' Robin. "

Rantin' Rovin' Robin'

" *may guid luck hit you* "

Lines To Mr John Kennedy

" *His uncomb'd grizzly locks, wild staring, thatch'd*
A head for thought profound and clear, unmatch'd;
Yet tho' his caustic wit was biting-rude,
His heart was warm, benevolent, and good. "

Mr William Smellie – A Sketch

**" *give me real, sterling wit,*
And I'm content "**

Epistle To James Smith

**" *Like brothers they'll stand by each other,*
Sae knit in alliance and kin. "**

Ballads on Mr Heron's Election, 1795

**" *Come to my bowl, come to my arms,*
My friends, my brothers! "**

Epistle To J Lapraik, An Old Scottish Bard

**" *Hale be your heart! Hale be your fiddle!*
Lang may your elbuck jink an' diddle, "**

Second Epistle to Davie

'I was na fou, but just had plenty'

Death And Doctor Hornbook

"The courtiers' gems may witness love,
But, 'tis na love like mine."

Behold, My Love, How Green The Groves

"Gin a body meet a body
Comin thro' the rye,
Gin a body kiss a body
Need a body cry."

Comin' Thro' The Rye

"Love enslaves the man"

Beware O' Bonie Ann

Selkirk Grace

Some Folk hae meat that canna eat,
And some can eat that want it;
But we hae meat, and we can eat,
So let the Lord be Thanket!

A Poet's Grace – Before Meat

O Thou who kindly dost provide
For every creature's want!
We bless Thee, God of Nature wide,
For all Thy goodness lent:
An' if it please Thee, Heavenly Guide,
May never worse be sent;
But, whether granted, or denied,
Lord, bless with us content.
Amen'

" *Wae worth thy pow'r, thou cursed leaf!*
Fell source o' a' my woe and grief!
For lack o' thee I've lost my lass,
For lack o' thee I scrimp my glass; "

Lines Written On A Banknote

"*My mirth and gude humour are coin in my pouch,
And my Freedom's my Lairdship nae monarch dare touch.*"

Contented Wi' Little And Cantie Wi' Mair

"*Though fickle Fortune has deceived me,
She promis'd fair and perform'd but ill,*"

Fickle Fortune

"*I make indeed my daily bread, but ne'er can make it farther, O;
But as daily bread is all I need, I do not much regard her, O.*"

My Father Was A Farmer

"What though on hamely fare we dine,
Wear hoddin grey, and a that;
Gie fools their silks, and knaves their wine,
A man's a man for a' that!
For a' that, and a' that,
Their tinsel show, and a' that;
The honest man, though e'er sae poor,
Is king o' men for a' that!,"

A Man's A Man For A' That

"Some, lucky, find a flow'ry spot,
For which they never toil'd nor swat;
They drink the sweet and eat the fat,"

Epistle To James Smith

Sandy and Jockie

Twa bony lads were Sandy and Jockie;
Jockie was lo'ed but Sandy unlucky;
Jockie was laird baith of hills and of vallies,
But Sandy was nought but the king o' gude fellows.
Jockie lo'ed Madgie, for Madgie had money,
And Sandie lo'ed Mary, for Mary was bony:
Ane wedded for Love, ane wedded for treasure,
So Jockie had siller, and Sandy had pleasure.

Man's inhumanity to man
Makes countless thousands mourn!

Man Was Made To Mourn: A Dirge

> **"What is title, what is treasure,
> What is reputation's care?
> If we lead a life of pleasure
> 'Tis no matter how or where!"**

The Jolly Beggars, or Love and Liberty – A Cantata

> **"Would thou hae Nobles' patronage?
> First learn to live without it!"**

Extempore On Some Commemorations of Thomson

> **"My laddie's sae meikle in luve wi' the siller,
> He canna hae luve to spare for me."**

My Tocher's the Jewel

"Now if ye're ane o' warl's folk,
Wha rate the wearer by the cloak,
An' sklent on poverty their joke,
W' bitter sneer,
Wi' you nae friendship I will troke,
Nor cheap nor dear."

To John Kennedy, Dumfries House

"How can your flinty hearts enjoy
The widow's tear, the orphan's cry?"

Logan Braes

O wad some Power
the giftie gie us
To see oursels as
ithers see us!

To A Louse

The heart benevolent
and kind
The most resembles
God

A Winter Night

"Lord help me thro' this warld o' care!"

Epistle To Dr Blacklock

"We seek but little, Lord, from thee,
Thou kens we get as little"

A New Psalm for the Chapel of Kilmarnock

"God knows, I'm no the thing I should be,
Nor am I even the thing I could be,
But twenty times I rather would be
An atheist clean,
Than under gospel colours hid be
Just for a screen."

To the Rev John McMath

"The minister kisst the fidler's wife,
He could na preach for thinking o't."

My Love, She's But A Lassie Yet

"*Altho' I'm not wi' Scripture cram'd,*
I'm sure the Bible says
That heedless sinners shall be damn'd,
Unless they mend their ways."

Epigram On Rough Roads

"*But yet, O Lord! confess I must,*
At times I'm fash'd w' fleshly lust;
And sometimes too, in wardly trust,
Vile self gets in;
But Thou remembers we are dust,
Defil'd wi' sin."

Holy Wullie's Prayer

" Hope not sunshine every hour,
Fear not clouds will always lour.
Happiness is but a name,
Make content and ease thy aim; "

Written In Friars Carse Hermitage, Nithsdale

" Happiness is but a name,
" I'll count my health my greatest wealth.
Sae lang as I'll enjoy it;
I'll fear nae scant, I'll bode nae want,
As lang's I get employment. "

Here's To Thy Health

" Contented wi' little, and cantie wi' mair "

Contented Wi' Little And Cantie Wi' Mair

**" Envy, if thy jaundiced eye
Though this window chance to spy,
To thy sorrow thou shalt find,
All that's generous, all that's kind,
Friendship, virtue, every grace,
Dwelling in this happy place. "**

At Whigham's Inn, Sanquhar

" Ne'er fash your head. "

Epistle To John Goldie, In Kilmarnock

" To make a happy fireside chime
To weans and wife,
That's the true pathos and sublime
Of human life. "

Epistle to Dr Blacklock

" The war'ly race may riches chase,
An' riches still may fly them, O
An' tho' at last they catch them fast,
Their hearts can ne'er enjoy them, O "

Green Grow The Rashes

"*Tell the truth and shame the deil*"

Versified Reply To An Invitation

**"*Believe me, happiness is shy,
And comes not aye when sought, man.*"**

A Bottle And A Friend

"*Life is but a day at most*"

Written In Friars Carse Hermitage, Nithsdale

"*An honest man's the noblest work of God!*"

The Cotter's Saturday Night

" they stretch an' strive:
Deil tak the hindmost! "

To A Haggis

" Sincere as a saint's dying prayer. "

Address To Wm. Tytler Esq of Woodhouselee

" Know, prudent, cautious, self-control
Is wisdom's root "

Epistle To John Goldie, In Kilmarnock

Time and Chance are but a tide

Duncan Gray

**" we're not to be bought and sold,
Like naigs, and nowt, and a' that. "**

Ballad on Mr Heron's Election – no. 1

**" You'll easy draw a lang-kent face,
But no sae weel a stranger "**

Epigram Addressed To An Artist

**" While we sing 'God save the King,'
We'll ne'er forget The People! "**

Does Haughty Gaul Invasion Threat?

**"*I never fash;*
I rhyme for fun."**

To James Smith

**"*Whene'er my Muse does on me glance,*
I jingle at her."**

Epistle to John Lapraik

**"*I winna blaw about mysel,*
As ill I like my fauts to tell;"**

Epistle To J Lapraik

"In manhood's various paths and ways
There's aye some doytin' body strays,
And I ride like the devil."

Election Ballad

"Gie me ae spark o' Nature's fire,
That's a' the learning I desire;"

Epistle to John Lapraik

"Come winter, with thine angry howl,
And raging, bend the naked tree;
Thy gloom will soothe my cheerless soul,
When nature all is sad like me!"

Composed In Spring

"*Fair fa' your honest, sonsie face,*
Great Chieftain o' the Puddin-race!
Aboon them a' ye tak your place,
Painch, tripe, or thairm:
Weel are ye wordy of a grace
As lang's my arm."

Address To A Haggis

"*Food fills the wame, an' keeps us leevin';*
Tho' life's a gift no worth receivin',
When heavy-dragg'd wi' pain an' grievin;
But, oil'd by thee,
The wheels o' life gae down-hill, scrievin',
Wi' rattlin' glee."

Scotch Drink

Wee, sleeket, cowran,
tim'rous beastie,

O, what a panic's
in thy breastie!

To A Mouse

"*My heart's in the Highlands, my heart is not here,*
My heart's in the Highlands, a-chasing the deer;
Chasing the wild-deer, and following the roe,
My heart's in the Highlands, wherever I go."

My Heart's In The Highlands

"*A lambkin in peace, but a lion in war*"

Caledonia – A Ballad

"*O Scotia! my dear, my native soil!*
For whom my warmest wish to Heaven is sent,"

The Cotter's Saturday Night

"*I am naebody's lord,*
I'll be slave to naebody;
I hae a gude braid sword,
I'll tak dunts frae naebody."

I Hae A Wife O' My Ain

"*Scots, wha hae wi' Wallace bled,*
Scots, wham Bruce has aften led,
Welcome to your gory bed –
Or to Victorie!"

Bruce's Address to his Army at Bannockburn

nocht can heal
my bosom's smart,

while, oh, she is
sae far awa!

My Native Land Sae Far Awa

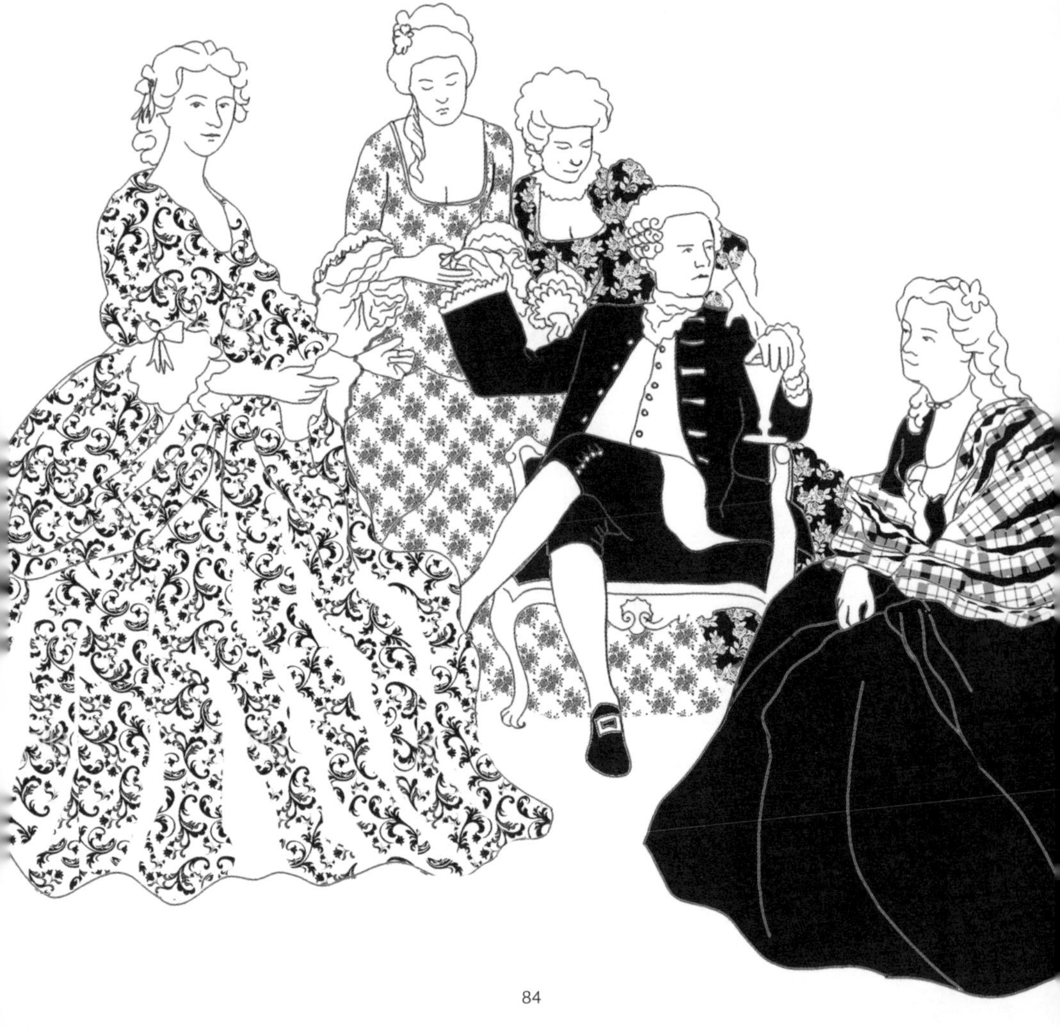

"He set his Jenny on his knee,
All in his Highland dress;
For brawly weel he ken'd the way
To please a bonnie lass!"

. . . .

"An' Charlie, he's my darling,
My darling, my darling,
Charlie, he's my darling,
The young Chevalier."

Charlie, he's my Darling

Auld Lang Syne

For auld lang syne, my dear,
For auld lang syne,
We'll tak a cup of kindness yet,
For auld lang syne!
Should auld acquaintance be forgot,
And never brought to mind?
Should auld acquaintance be forgot,
And auld lang syne?
And surely ye'll be your pint-stowp,
And surely I'll be mine,
And we'll tak a cup o kindness yet,
For auld lang syne!

We twa hae run about the braes,
And pou'd the gowans fine,
But we've wander'd monie a weary fit,
Sin auld lang syne.
We twa hae paidl'd in the burn
Frae morning sun till dine,
But seas between us braid hae roar'd
Sin auld lang syne.
And there's a hand my trusty fiere,
And gie's a hand o thine,
And we'll tak a right guid-willie waught,
For auld lang syne.

Now's the day,
and now's the hour;

Bruce's Address to his Army at Bannockburn

**" Love, thou hast pleasure, and deep hae I lov'd;
Love, thou hast sorrows, and sair hae I prov'd:
But this bruised heart that now bleeds in my breast,
I can feel by its throbbings will soon be at rest. "**

Wae Is My Heart

**" But till we meet and weet our whistle,
Tak this excuse for nae epistle. "**

Epistle To Hugh Parker

" *When Death's dark stream I ferry o'er,*
A time that surely shall come,
In Heav'n itself I'll ask no more,
Than just a Highland welcome. "

Epigram On Parting With A Kind Host In The Highlands

" *saint or sinner,*
Rob the Ranter "

Epistle To James Tennant of Glenconner

" *And gratefully, my gude auld cockie,*
I'm yours for aye.
Robert Burns "

Epistle To Dr Blacklock

Robert Burns

Glossary

aft	often
auld	old
bickerin'	hurrying/noisy argument
billies	comrades/friends
billows	loudly
blethers	talk nonsense
bode	look for
body	person
bonie/bony	pretty/beautiful
brae	slope of a hill
braid	broad
breastie	breast
cantie	cheerful/jolly
chapman	salesman
cowran	cowering
cumbrous	commotion
deil	devil
dow	be able to date/a dove
doytin'	doddering
dunts	blows
e'e/een	eye/eyes
fash	trouble/worry/an annoyance

fierce	sound/active
fou	drunk
fu'	full/drunk
gang	go
gie	give
gin	if/whether/should/by
gowans	wild/mountain daisy
Gude	God
guid	good
guid-willie	full of goodwill
hae	have
hale	healthy/whole
hoddin'	riding heavily
ilka	each and every
ithers	others
kirk	church
lang	long
lang-kent	long known
lang syne	long since/long ago
lassie	girl/lady/term of endearment
lo'e	love
mony	many
na	no
naig	horse
nappy	strong ale
neebors	neighbours
nocht	nothing
nowt	cattle

paidl'd	paddle/wade
painch	paunch
pou'd	to pull
rin	to run
sair	sore/sad/aching
scrimp	scanty
siller	silver/money
sklent	slant/glance/squint
sleekit	crafty/sly
snaw	snow
sonsie	pleasant/plump/cheerful
swat	sweated
thairn	belly of man/beast/fiddle string
the gither	together
thou	you
tim'rous	timid
trinkling	flowing
troke	barter/exchange
unco	uncommon/strange/extremely unusual
wad	wager/marry
warld	world
waught	big drink/copious draught
wee	small
weel	well
wrang	wrong